D0554801

The Electronic
Music Scene

The Stars ♪ The Fans ♪ The Music

Jessica Cohn

Enslow Publishers, Inc.
40 Industrial Road
Box 398
Berkeley Heights, NJ 07922
USA

http://www.enslow.com

Library of Congress Cataloging-in-Publication Data
Cohn, Jessica.
  The electronic music scene : the stars, the fans, the music / Jessica Cohn.
    p. cm. — (The music scene)
  Includes bibliographical references and index.
  Summary: "Read about the music, stars, clothes, contracts, and world of electronic
music"—Provided by publisher.
  ISBN-13: 978-0-7660-3398-6
  ISBN-10: 0-7660-3398-8
  1. Underground dance music—History and criticism—Juvenile literature. I. Title.
  ML3540.5.C64 2009
  782.42164—dc22

                              2008048012

Printed in the United States of America

10 9 8 7 6 5 4 3 2 1

To Our Readers:
This text has not been authorized by the musicians or bands mentioned throughout
this book.
    We have done our best to make sure all Internet addresses in this book were
active and appropriate when we went to press. However, the author and the publisher
have no control over and assume no liability for the material available on those
Internet sites or on other Web sites they may link to. Any comments or suggestions
can be sent by e-mail to comments@enslow.com or to the address on the back cover.

♻ Enslow Publishers, Inc., is committed to printing our books on recycled paper.
The paper in every book contains 10% to 30% post-consumer waste (PCW). The
cover board on the outside of each book contains 100% PCW. Our goal is to do our
part to help young people and the environment too!

Cover Photo Credit: Shutterstock
Interior Photo Credits: Alamy/Tristan O'Neill/PYMCA, p. 9; Alamy/Jim Size, p. 16;
Alamy/Picture Partners, p. 19; Alamy/Real World People, p. 28;
Alamy/Rene Paik, p. 38; Alamy/CuboImages srl,
p. 41; AP Photo/Jacques Brinon, p. 11; AP Photo/
Kevin P. Casey, p. 18; Getty Images/Paul Warner/
WireImage, p. 25; iStockphoto.com/Robert Kohlhuber,
p. 1; Jupiter Images/James Lange/PYMCA, p. 8; Alex
Kaplan/alexkaplanphotography.com/Courtesy of Renée
Zawawi, p. 33; Landov/Rubra/Reuters, p. 6; Landov/Jean-Paul
Pelissier/Reuters, p. 10; Landov/Didier Saulnier/Maxppp, p. 12;
Landov/John Angelillo, p. 26 (right); Landov/Lucy Nicholson/
Reuters, p. 31; MPTVIMAGES.COM/Dream Works, pp. 22–23; Courtesy
NextAid [www.nextaid.org], pp. 36, 37; Retna Ltd./Joshua Prezant, pp. 2,
5, 26 (left); Retna Ltd./Timothy Cochrane, p. 7; Retna Ltd./Robb D. Cohen,
p. 14; Retna Ltd./Rob Hann/Retna UK, p. 15; Retna Ltd./Tina Paul/Camera
Press, p. 17; Retna Ltd./Amanda Rose, p. 20; Retna Ltd./Rahav Segev, p. 21;
Retna Ltd./Dominik Gigler/Vanit, p. 34; Retna Ltd./Timothy Saccenti, p. 35.

Cover: Fans go wild at a concert.
Title page: Dancers move under
the lights at a club.
Right: A DJ gets fans going at the
Ultra Music Festival in Miami.

Contents

1 *Hot Stuff*

When people started making music with electronics, magic started happening. Suddenly musicians could make any sounds they wanted! There were no limits.

What Is *Electronic Music?*

Electronic music, or electronica, is music made with electronic equipment. Many artists use electronics for everything—from the beat to the instruments to the extra noise. Other artists mix electronics with regular instruments or a choir. It depends on the feeling they are going for.

Filling *Our Ears*

Electronica is everywhere. You hear it on movie soundtracks, such as *Transformers* (2007). You hear it in video games like *Spore*. It's in the music of pop artists such as **Beck**, **Bjork**, **Moby**, and **Kylie Minogue**.

DJ Tiesto plays live in Miami.

Electronica's Annual "Meeting"

The Miami Winter Music Conference is an annual "who's who" of electronica. Stars like **DJ Tiesto**, **Justice**, and **Underworld** have played there. You can also find artists like **Paul van Dyk** and **Audiofly**. Each year, about two hundred artists, DJs, and producers come together to celebrate.

At shows like the Miami Winter Music Conference, you hear a wilderness of sound. Some of the songs are made for dancing, while other songs help you think. There's so much happening, it's easy to get lost in it. Electronica's next biggest fan—or star—just might be you.

Fans gather along the Danube River in Austria to hear the electronic music of Peter Wolf.

2 "I'm Your Biggest Fan!"

In the 1970s and 1980s, electronica built a big fan base in "underground" American dance clubs. Early electronica fans were people who danced to disco. Later waves of fans were mostly young people who wanted to hear the newest club music.

Raves and warehouse parties attracted huge crowds in the 1980s and 1990s. At these events, it was too loud to talk much. People moved to the music instead.

In Every Space

Teens cut loose in the basements of big city churches. They bobbed to the beat in dance halls. Young people hung out in huge spaces filled with flashing lights. With everybody moving and tightly packed, it was easy to imagine the crowd as one being. It was harder to think of people alone in their shells.

Out from Under

Many electronic music artists got by independently—or "underground"—with no help from major record companies. Their popularity came from word of mouth. Over time, electronica entered the mainstream. Name a type of music—rap, country, pop, hip-hop, or even classical. Electronic technology has influenced each type. Today, electronic music reaches nearly all music fans.

A crowded show in London brings fans together.

③ *Ultimate Style*

When you want to dance all night long, you need comfortable clothes. Dancers at early raves looked for easy-to-wear outfits that also stood out. They wore spandex, lycra, and other stretchy and shiny materials. These fabrics clung to the body and made it easier to move.[1] A lot of rock musicians performing at that time, such as *David Bowie*, had the same kind of style.

Specific looks developed in different places. In California, where the personal computer was born, music and electronics were blended early. Many fans of West Coast bands carried on with the hippie looks of the 1960s—headbands and colorful shirts. For a while, dancers in London wore chemical protection masks. Some people wore white gloves.

Name something that glows in the dark, and you'll find an electronica fan wearing it!

Today's "Look"

Today, the "look" doesn't have any rules. It's about being comfortable and expressing yourself.[2] Some fans wear jeans and T-shirts, while others stand out with a silly hat or a wild haircut. The T-shirts might have in-your-face sayings on them. They might make fun of popular brand names.[3]

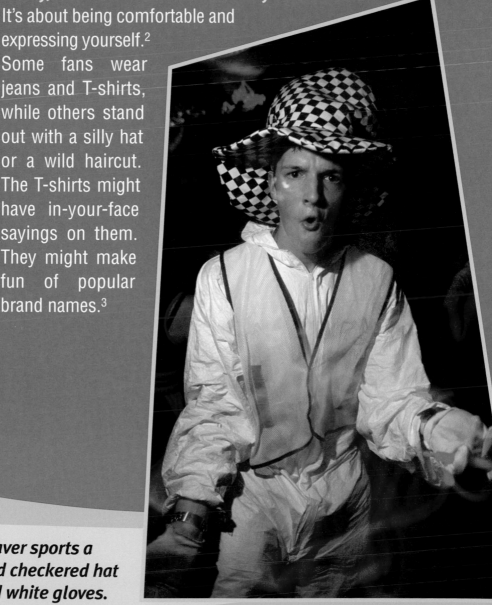

A raver sports a wild checkered hat and white gloves.

9

Fancy Flyers

Today, promoters can send out text messages to advertise a dance event. But before people carried cell phones, promoters used flyers. Artists put a lot of work into flyers that would attract big crowds. Early 1990s dance club flyers often had a hippie vibe, with bright colors and wavy lines. New York clubs' flyers looked like modern art.

Outfitted

For fans of EDM—electronic dance music—style is about more than just clothing. The new craze called Tck, or vertigo, is a good example. In the Tck look, guys often wear ducktails in their hair. Many dancers look gothic or punk, and they wave glow-in-the-dark gloves. Fans favor black. They wear jeans and jackets with a 1950s flair.

A Tck fan gets a punk haircut with a ducktail in back. The Tck trend has spread quickly in the world of electronica.

Tck dancers do "hip-hop, techno, and aerobics," notes one reporter in Paris.[4] Their dancing becomes a performance art. Tck performers meet in clubs at night and dance together. They do dance battles on the streets during the day.

A Tck dancer performs on a street in Paris during the Techno Parade in September 2007.

4 Dance!

Plenty of **electronica** is for at-home listening, but EDM is all about dancing.

All About the Beat

A steady beat fills the room. It pounds in the dancers' hearts. Their feet thump along to the music, and they move with their mood. The crowd moves in waves. For a while, one dancer seems to take a partner . . . but then turns away. The music encourages individual movements. Yet people also feel like they're part of something larger. The whole crowd has its own dance going on.

A dance club is like a big stage. DJs fill video screens with moving pictures. Patterns of light move across the walls, floors, and ceilings. Dancers use props as if they're in a play—light sticks, horns, and other objects.

Anything Goes

In EDM, just about anything goes. For example, Tck dancers move their arms in a blur. Then they slow down and draw out their movements as if they are stretching. They spin, jump, and bend—anything to expand into the space around, above, and below them. Anything to get attention!

In electronica, the music tells you what to do. Some dancers just close their eyes and listen. Then they feel their bodies start to move.

Live concerts are a challenge for the Chicago band Tortoise. There are too many instruments and too few people to play them!

5 On the Road

Electronic musicians could easily stay in the studio, but they might lose their edge. So performers push to go on tour, even though playing live is a challenge.

Three Places at the Same Time

The Chicago band **Tortoise** puts their songs together in a studio. "When we go out to play the stuff live," guitarist Jeff Parker says, "we have to learn it from the recordings."[5] In a studio song, one band member might play three different instruments at three different times and then put them together later. In live concerts, the musicians sometimes have to scramble to cover all the parts. But fans say there is nothing better than seeing Tortoise live.

The Biggest Shows

In 2007, the French duo *Justice* was the main act for the MySpace Music Tour. They ended with a show at Madison Square Garden in New York City. Until that year, Justice had been playing mainly mid-size clubs.[6] "It was a little stressful because we are using new equipment, but in general people were happy," says band member *Gaspard Augé*.[7]

When the British duo *Digweed* toured North America in 2008, they purposely played at smaller clubs. They said, "[We] really wanted to go back to our underground roots. ... Recently the only shows we have done together have been massive festival events. So this time around we are playing ... clubs with great sound systems rather than big arena shows, which will give our fans a chance to see us in a more intimate environment."[8]

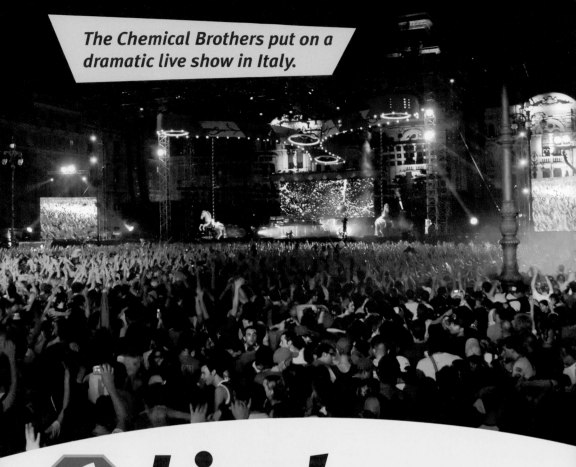

6 Live!

Nothing compares to live electronica. When *Kraftwerk* played at the Coachella Music and Arts Festival in 2008, the musicians stood behind laptops while music pumped through the air. Flashing lights created cutouts of standing figures against a darkened sky. The crowd pounded the air with their fists. The beat took over.

The Live Connection

It is one thing to listen to an MP3 player, and quite another to be part of the crowd. Fans and musicians connect through shared sights and sounds. Some fans follow their favorite performers for years.

The Chemical Brothers—Tom Rowlands and *Ed Simons*—first played live at a sweaty dance spot in London. By 1999, they filled Red Rocks Stadium in Colorado. There were thousands of fans. The scene included food stands, security guards, and souvenir shops.[9] Today, their tours take them all over the globe.

Finding a Show

Electronica fans can enjoy music at small clubs in Minneapolis, Nashville, or wherever they call home. Or they can try larger, shared experiences, like the Underworld Show in New York City's Central Park. Thousands of fans gather under the stars and dance, surrounded by forest.

Karl Hyde of the band Underworld performs at the annual Underworld Show in Central Park.

7 Ear Candy

Most American radio stations are not big on electronica. They usually don't play electronic music unless it's a crossover act, like songs on **Madonna**'s album *Ray of Light*. Even when U.S. stations play electronic music, it's usually at an off time, such as early Sunday morning. You'll hear a lot more electronica on major stations in Asia, Europe, and South America. To enjoy nonstop electronica, you can tune in to satellite radio or online stations.

It is difficult to find electronic music on mainstream American radio stations.

Calling It Your Own

Fans can hit a record store and sample the electronic music section. Many fans download music files from iTunes and other online music stores. They also look for music on the performers' Web sites.

Large music stores have a selection of electronic music and videos on CD and DVD.

Hyperreal

One fantastic source of electronica is the Internet library Hyperreal, started at Stanford University in 1992. Before home computers, you had to go to a university to use collections like this. With Hyperreal, you can hear songs from all over the world with one click of your mouse.

Keeping It Legal
MP3 technology lets people download songs in seconds. Taking downloads from an honest and legal site is OK. But when you share files or burn music onto CDs, it is usually illegal. Musicians deserve to be paid. Get your music the legal way.

⑧ *Hottest Videos*

In 1994, *Future Sound of London (FSOL)* gave fans *ISDN,* a live album that included images. When you think of a live album, you usually think of music recorded at a concert in front of fans. FSOL twisted the idea. The musicians fed their new songs live to radio stations around the world. They used ISDN (digital telephone) lines. These feeds are usually used for news. The musicians were able to

send the images, printed words, and artwork along with the music. Then these performances were recorded for the album.

New Ideas

In 2006, FSOL was still playing with new ways to

On MTV, you can find videos of the popular electronica crossover act Moby.

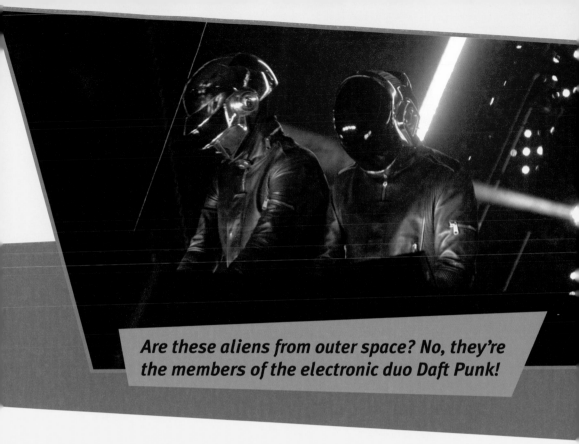

Are these aliens from outer space? No, they're the members of the electronic duo Daft Punk!

communicate with fans. They released music that went with a DVD—and a video that fans could download—in *Future Music Magazine*.[10]

MTV and Beyond

Electronic music artists often push their video projects in new directions. You can tune your TV to major video stations like MTV or VH1. There, you can see crossover acts, like **Moby** or even **Madonna**. The best place for the hottest new electronic music videos, however, is on the Web. On YouTube, you can see all kinds of performers, from **Daft Punk** to **M.I.A.**

9 Electronica in Movies and TV

Electronica is very common in Hollywood. Even soundtracks that do not feature electronica have elements of it. Just listen to the music in the movie *Transformers* (2007).

On the Big Screen

Electronic artist **Paul Haslinger** has brought his talents to movies. He mixes electronica with classical music to help move stories along. You can hear his work in *Blue Crush* (2002) and *Underworld* (2003).[11]
Science fiction movies have featured electronica since the 1950s. Musicians use instruments such as the theremin to make spooky sounds. A recent sci-fi film with electronic music is *Alien vs. Predator* (2004).

On the Small Screen

TV shows are filled with electronica. Just watch the animated series *Futurama*. Creator Matt Groening even built his own theremin!

Many video games are also set to electronic music. As players click their way through games like *Doom*, they hear some of the best in electronica. When the game *Spore* came out in 2008, YouTube featured a music video of **Brian Eno**'s electronic music score.

Chip music, or bit boxing, is music made using electronic sounds from video games. One New York "game sound artist" called **Bubblyfish** went on five tours of Europe in one year alone.

The soundtrack of the 2007 movie *Transformers is filled with electronica.*

10 A First Moment

High Tech Soul (2006) is a movie about the early electronic music scene in Detroit, Michigan. Detroit is known as the birthplace of the Motown sound, yet Motown was just act one. Act two was techno. Techno is a form of EDM with machine beats. It usually has no voices.

Back in Belleville

High Tech Soul is about **Juan Atkins**, **Derrick May**, and **Kevin Saunderson**. They met in a suburb of Detroit called Belleville. The town didn't have many blacks. Together, the three African-American teens would listen to music and think about life after high school. "We'd sit back with the lights off and listen to records by **Bootsy** and **Yellow Magic Orchestra**," May says. "We never took it as entertainment. We took it as serious philosophy."[12]

The song "Good Vibrations" (1966), by the Beach Boys, became the first pop hit that was considered electronic.

Techno Is Born

The **Belleville Three**, as the young men would come to be called, became DJs in the 1980s. They broke into the Detroit party scene with their own form of electronica: techno. Then they surged into the mainstream. "Oddly enough," writes Dan Sicko in *Techno Rebels*, "this would happen not in other regions of the United States, but rather across the Atlantic in the U.K."[13] Virgin Records asked the Belleville Three to record in London. The rest is history.

Derrick May, a member of the Belleville Three, spins at a show in Detroit in 2008.

The talents of DJ Tiesto (left) and pop star Justin Timberlake combined for a hot remix of Timberlake's song "Lovestoned."

11 Not So Simple

As electronic music trips through time, it changes. It develops hybrids, or blends. Artists struggle with songs. Should they add more rhythm or harmony? Is it time for some noise? Sometimes they stumble onto something really new.

Time for Something New
The music also changes in response to other artists and fans. An artist hears something new

and answers with something that is just different enough to be called something else.

Musicians also work together to create fresh new styles. That special kind of energy happened when *DJ Tiesto*, a trance DJ, remixed *Justin Timberlake*'s song "Lovestoned" (2007).

Types of
Electronic Music

There are way too many types of electronica to list here, but these are a few types with staying power:[14]

- ♪ *Ambient*—a "roomy" sound, with lots of texture and repetition. *Brian Eno* does ambient.
- ♪ *Drum and bass*—has fast rhythms and break beats; think *Photek*.
- ♪ *House*—music with mechanical beats, deep bass, and fewer vocals than many other forms; think DJs. The city of Chicago claims it is the home of house.
- ♪ *Techno*—music meant for "listening" audiences, but has a hardcore dance version as well; the music of *Kraftwerk* stands out.
- ♪ *Trance*—uses repetition of synthesizers to put listeners in a trance. *Paul van Dyke* is a master.
- ♪ *Industrial*—a distorted form of music that brings in heavy metal performers; these are often underground performers, such as *Chrome*.

Electronic music is all about new technology. Here, a woman uses a synthesizer hooked up to a computer in a recording studio.

12 *Plugged In*

What makes ambient different from industrial? Techno from drum and bass? It's the way the artists play with electronics. It's what they want you to get from it—something relaxing or something that gets you dancing.

Synthesize!

The basic tool of electronica is the synthesizer. A synthesizer is a machine that creates hundreds of different sounds. The first electric synthesizer was made in 1876. Classical musicians have been playing with electronic instruments for a long time. What *is* new is the way musicians use synthesizers.

In 1968, Robert Moog made the Moog synthesizer. This machine could move from place to place more easily than earlier machines. More musicians started to play with electronic sound. In the 1980s, Yamaha and other companies started making electronic keyboards. Even more people could afford to buy them. That is when MIDI, or musical instrument digital interface, became popular. With MIDI, you can make entire electronic songs on your home computer.

At-Home DJs

Today, many different electronic tools can make and mix sounds. The home computer has created a revolution in music. You can become a DJ in your own living room!

⬡13 *The Studios*

Electronic musicians have been pioneers in the way music is produced. Most have survived without help from the major studios. The big five studios—BMG, EMI, Sony, Universal, and Warner—have some electronic musicians on contract. But most electronic music acts are independent.

The Independents

Independent record studios mix and package most electronic music. These companies form and fall apart regularly, but some—such as Astralwerks—have stuck around. Independent labels often work together to promote their artists. They group together on Web sites to get their artists more attention.

Radiohead Bucks the System

The influence of the studios is changing. For example, consider *Radiohead*. They are considered an alternative rock band, but they are also electronic.

For years, Radiohead had an agreement with the major studio EMI. But when the contract ended after their sixth album, Radiohead decided to go out on their own. **Thom Yorke**, the band's lead vocalist, said that working with a studio was "a decaying business model."[15] Radiohead's seventh album, *In Rainbows*, was released on the Web as a digital download. Radiohead did what no other hit band had done before. They asked fans to name the price they would pay for the album. The experiment was an enormous success: *In Rainbows* won a Grammy for 2008.

Thom Yorke and the band Radiohead perform at the 51st Grammy Awards in 2009. Radiohead went home with a Grammy for their album **In Rainbows.**

14 Tale of a "Contract"

Electronic musicians became pioneers of managing their careers. They started asking themselves, "Why wait for a big studio when you can sign yourself?" Electronic musicians like to take their music directly to the people.

It Starts with a Demo

Here is the story of **Renée Zawawi**. This electronic artist released the popular album *L-E-G-E-N-D-S* in 2007. She started a new Web site and a MySpace promotion featuring her single "American Girrrl." She sent out press packets. Soon she had a YouTube video and her own ringtone, along with several positive Web reviews.

Zawawi hired the Demo Center, in New York City, to help produce her first recording. Production spaces like the Demo Center help new artists make a music sampler. Then the artists take the sampler to record labels.

Making the Investment

A demo is like an investment in yourself. "Making an album can costs thousands and thousands of dollars," says Demo Center producer Cary Scope. Instead, a demo might cost two thousand dollars and include only three songs. "You come to us if you're going to try to shop it [the demo] at a record label," he says.[16] After making her demo, Zawawi went on to record an entire album.

To make her first album, Renée Zawawi skipped the recording studios and awarded herself a "contract."

Photek (Rupert Parkes) is the king of drum and bass.

15 Take One!

The music business can seem glamorous, but it takes hard work to make a recording. You need a lot of time and creative ideas.

Photek

Just ask **Rupert Parkes**. Some people know him as the Sentinel. Others know him as Studio Pressure. He is called Aquarius and many other names. Yet the name that makes most people sit up and take notice is **Photek**. He is the king of drum and bass.

Parkes became successful and built himself a recording studio. He does a lot of work there alone, but he is not a one-man band all the time. When working on a project with the group *TV on the Radio*, Parkes headed to New York. The artists spent hours getting to know one another and building the music.

"There are always issues when integrating into another studio," said Parkes. "One of the coolest moments, creatively speaking, was when we all went out at midnight and set up the drum kit in the street and [the drummer] slammed out a load of different patterns for about half an hour. We recorded from three different sources—cassette recorder, DV camera, DAT—at different distances. The natural reverb from the street and buildings was amazing."[17]

Photek and the band TV on the Radio (shown here) got creative inside—and outside—the studio.

16 *Electronic Music in Action*

Many electronica artists believe in giving back to the public. Some of them donate money and time to struggling musicians. In 2006, electronic musicians participated at the Gathering in Philadelphia. It was organized to benefit the Innovative Music and Arts in Pennsylvania.

On an even wider scale, electronic artists perform at NextAid Miami. This annual event is held at clubs all over Miami. Like all of NextAid's activities, it benefits children in Africa, such as orphans whose parents died from AIDS.

Mark Farina, a world-famous DJ and producer, and recording artist Anna Song show their support for NextAid at the 2006 Winter Music Conference in Miami. At events like these, members of the electronic music community work together for the good of the world.

NextAid Up Close

NextAid is based in Los Angeles, but it helps run musical events all around the country. Musicians who join NextAid help bring attention to the problems in Africa. They try to find people who have solutions to the problems. They link people who want to help through the arts and public education.

One NextAid project is building a village in South Africa. The village will house fifty children and serve a thousand people in the surrounding area. It will include a business center and a performance space and gardens.

San Francisco hosts an annual NextAid event called For the Kids. It, too, brings together the international electronic music community for the good of children in need.

A keyboard is your passport into the world of electronica.

17 Get into It

Now that you know all about electronica, find a way to get involved! Some musicians start out by playing with an electronic keyboard or guitar.

Set Up Your Studio

There are three basic home studio setups. Some people prefer portable digital studios. These are basically desktop recorders that use a computer. Other people are comfortable with

Mac- or Windows-based software. Audacity is a free program that can work for either Mac or PC. Programs such as Reaper, Podium, Mixcraft, and Sony's Acid Express can be downloaded for a fee. Other musicians work away from the computer with hard disk recorders, mixers, and outboard gear.[18]

Here's the key: don't spend too much money at first. You will learn more as you go along. Research your options. Read magazines, like *Electronic Musician* online, and check out electronic music books at the library

You can also try an online tutorial. A tutorial guides you through the steps of moving from one piece of equipment or software to another.

Expert Advice

A variety of music schools, colleges, and universities offer classes in recording music. You could also try contacting a production house in your area and asking if anyone is willing to teach you. Before you know it, you could be streaming your music in a podcast or posting a video on YouTube. You could even enter an electronic music contest like those held by Broadjam or Billboard.com.

18 *For a Living*

An interest in electronic music can turn into a long-term career. There are many jobs besides being a DJ or other performer. You could be a music writer or producer. You could work in a studio for a major or independent record company.

Sound *Designer*

A music synthesist is someone trained to design sounds. In this job, you could work with a composer to produce music for the Internet. Or you might work at a TV or film studio to help with soundtracks.

Pick Up *Your Pen*

In the arts, you might enjoy being a music editor, writer, or critic. A college degree in music and writing will help.

Be a Techie

If the "toys" of electronica attract you, there are plenty of jobs for electronic repair people. Many U.S. factories and laboratories need highly qualified electronic techs.

Electronic Therapy

In health, you can work as a music therapist. These professionals help people recover from long-lasting illness by developing their enjoyment of music.

Whatever field interests you, follow where it leads! Electronica will be around for a long time.

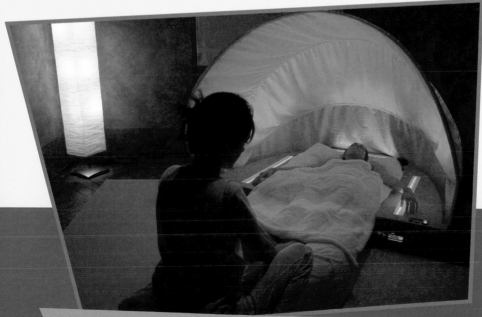

A music therapist plays relaxing melodies for a client.

Glossary

aerobics—A kind of dancelike exercise that temporarily speeds up your breathing rate and heart rate.

alternative rock—Rock music with rap, punk, heavy metal, and other elements.

archive—A place where records are kept.

break beats—Beats without the usual steady rhythm.

chemical protection masks—Face coverings that keep people from breathing harmful substances.

decaying—Rotting away; dying.

demo—A sample recording of a musician's work.

disco—Popular dance music of the 1970s.

DJs—People who play and mix albums at a club or electronica show.

electronic technology—Machines, such as synchronizers, powered by the movement of electrons.

hard disk recorders—Machines that record music to a computer disk.

hybrids—Blends of two or more styles.

intimate—Close and personal.

mainstream—Popular culture that the majority of people know about.

mixers—Machines that combine different sounds.

Motown—A kind of music that rose out of gospel music in Detroit, Michigan.

outboard gear—Music equipment, such as a compressor or an equalizer, that helps people mix sounds.

performance art—Art that includes staged, dramatic, often surprising elements.

producers—In music, people who create a musical act or recording, either by paying for it or arranging to get it done.

promoters—People who organize events and spread the word about them.

raves—Large electronic dance parties.

synthesizer—A machine used to produce sound or to copy the sounds of musical instruments.

synthetic—Made of human-made materials.

texture—The "touchable" quality that you get when you put lots of elements together.

tutorial—A brief, step-by-step system of instruction.

Time Line

1897 The telharmonium, an early electronic musical instrument, is invented. This machine could send music over telephone lines.

1900 The age of electronic music begins.

1919–1920 Léon Theremin invents the theremin, the first electronic instrument played without touching the instrument.

1950s Rock 'n' roll is born.

1960s Motown is born, and rock becomes more electronic.

1964 The Moog synthesizer is invented.

1967 The Beach Boys' "Good Vibrations" becomes the first pop hit featuring electronica.

1970s The age of electronic dance music begins.

1980s The age of computers and electronics begins.

1983 MIDI (musical instrument digital interface) is invented.

1984 Disco becomes house music.

1986 Detroit techno takes off.

1990s Electronic dance forms, such as new age, ambient, and jungle, continue to branch off.

2005 Until Spring Revisited, the first classical concert performed on only a laptop, opens in New York City.

2006 YouTube starts providing electronic music and videos for the Internet masses.

2008 SoundCloud launches a music-sharing platform, allowing musicians to share tracks without cluttering e-mail.

2009 A. R. Rahman, composer for the film *Slumdog Millionaire*, wins Oscars for best movie score and song. His mix of electronic and Indian music speaks to a world of new listeners. What will be next?

End Notes

1. Pauline Weston Thomas, "1960–1980 Fashion History," *Fashion-Era.com*, n.d., <http://www.fashion-era.com/1960-1980.htm> (March 15, 2008).

2. Gail Robertson, "All the Rave," *The Windsor Star*, May 18, 1993, p. C01.

3. Sam Knight, "Hope You Saved Your Glow Stick," *New York Times*, January 21, 2007, <http://www.nytimes.com/2007/01/21/fashion/21Rave.html> (March 3, 2009).

4. Robert Marquand, "It's techno with a Parisian twist—a lot of crazy twists," *Christian Science Monitor*, January 29, 2008, p.1.

5. Will Layman, "A *Lazarus Taxon*: the Definition of 'Tortoise' Continues to Change Before Our Eyes," *PopMatters*, August 21, 2006, <http://www.popmatters.com/music/interviews/tortoise-060821.shtml> (March 3, 2009).

6. "Justice to Headline MySpace Music Tour," *Spin*, January 9, 2008, <http://spin.com/articles/justice-headline-myspace-music-tour> (March 15, 2008).

7. Becca Nelson, "Justice: Interview with Gaspard Auge," *Reax Music Magazine*, February 1, 2008, <http://www.reaxmusic.com/articles/view/justice_interview_with_gaspard_aug-480> (March 3, 2009).

8. Sotek, "Sasha & John Digweed tour North America," *Filter27*, February 22, 2008, <http://www.filter27.com/archives/2008/02/sasha-john-digweed-2008-tour.php> (March 3, 2009).

9. "The Chemical Brothers Biography," *Y! MUSIC*, n.d., <http://search.music.yahoo.com/search/?m=all&p=chemical+brothers> (March 3, 2009).

10. Colin Larkin, ed., *The Encyclopedia of Popular Music* (London: Omnibus Press, 2007), p. 572.

11. Mr. Bonzai, "From Tangerine Dream to the Big Screen," *Electronic Musician*, March 1, 2006, <http://emusician.com/mag/emusic_tangerine_dream_big/> (March 3, 2009).

12. Simon Reynolds, *Generation Ecstasy* (New York: Little, Brown and Company, 1998), p.15.

13. Dan Sicko, *Techno Rebels: The Renegades of Electronic Funk* (New York: Billboard Books, 1999), p. 96.

14. "Electronic Music Styles," *Analogik*, n.d., <http://analogik.com/res_styles.asp> (March 3, 2009).

15. Josh Tyrangiel, "Radiohead Says: Pay What You Want," *TIME*, October 1, 2007, <http://www.time.com/time/arts/article/0,8599,1666973,00.html> (March 3, 2009).

16. Jessica Cohn, personal phone interview with Cary Scope, March 1, 2008.

17. Kylee Swenson, "Exclusive Interview with Photek!" *Remix*, January 11, 2006, <http://remixmag.com/transmissions/photek-011206/> (March 3, 2009).

18. Steve O, "How to Build a Personal Studio on Any Budget," *Electronic Musician*, July 1, 2002, <http://emusician.com/tutorials/emusic_build_personal_studio/> (March 3, 2009).

Further Reading

Books

Fassbender, Torsten. *The Trance Experience: An Introduction to Electronic Dance Music.* Knoxville, Tenn.: Sound.org, 2005.

Preve, Francis. *The Remixer's Bible: Build Better Beats.* San Francisco: Backbeat Books, 2006.

Snoman, Rick. *Dance Music Manual: Toys, Tools and Techniques.* Burlington, Mass.: Focal Press, 2004.

Web Sites

Analogik—A place to learn about electronic music, find new artists, and download hot new songs
<http://analogik.com>

Electronic Music Magazine—Find out the latest news in the electronic music community
<http://www.emusician.com>

Keyboard Magazine—Explore the keyboard's contribution to music around the world
<http://www.keyboardmag.com>

Index